Recipes from
China

Dana Meachen Rau

Raintree

Chicago, Illinois

Edited by Abby Colich, Laura Knowles, and
    John-Paul Wilkins
Designed by Cynthia Akiyoshi
Picture research by Tracy Cummins
Production by Vicki Fitzgerald
Originated by Capstone Global Library
Printed and bound in China by Leo Paper
    Products Ltd

17 16 15 14 13
10 9 8 7 6 5 4 3 2 1

**Library of Congress Cataloging-in-
Publication Data**
Rau, Dana Meachen, 1971-
  Recipes from China / Dana M. Rau.
    pages cm.—(Cooking around the
world)
  Includes bibliographical references and
index.
  ISBN 978-1-4109-5971-3 (hardback)
 1. Cooking, Chinese—Juvenile literature.
I. Title.

TX724.5.C5R38 2014
641.5951—dc23   2013017269

Acknowledgments
The author and publisher are grateful to
the following for permission to reproduce
copyright material: Capstone Publishers
pp. 1, 9–11, 16–43 (Karon Dubke);
ChooseMyPlate.gov p. 12 (with thanks to
USDA's Center for Nutrition Policy and
Promotion); Getty Images pp. 7 (blue jean
images), 15 (Lena Granefelt); Shutterstock
p. 4 (Kang Khoon Seang), 5 (TonyV3112),
6 (ValeStock), 13 (Monkey Business Images),
14 (Karlova Irina).

Design elements reproduced with
permission of Shutterstock (Andrew
Scherbackov, Andrey Zyk, Brooke Becker,
Evlakhov Valeriy, Fedorov Oleksiy, Flavia
Morlachetti, K13 ART, Luis Santos,
HUANSHENG XU, marchello74, Mazzzur,
Muellek Josef, Ninell, Oleg_Z, photastic,
Picsfive, Richard Peterson, Sandra
Cunningham, spaxiax, TungCheung).

Cover photograph of tofu with pea pods
and bamboo shoots reproduced with
permission of Capstone Publishers (Karon
Dubke).

We would like to thank Seth Wiener,
Sarah Schenker, and Marla Conn for their
invaluable help in the preparation of this
book.

Every effort has been made to contact
copyright holders of any material
reproduced in this book. Any omissions will
be rectified in subsequent printings if notice
is given to the publisher.

Contents

Large Country, Long History

China is a large country covering much of southern Asia. In fact, China is the third-largest country in land area in the world. In the north, it borders Russia and Mongolia. The west and south border many countries, including India, Nepal, Myanmar (Burma), and Vietnam. The eastern edge is a coastline along the Pacific Ocean. Since China covers such a large land area, the country contains many different types of land. The Himalayas loom over China's southwest border, and contain some of the world's highest peaks. Dry deserts cover parts of the northwest. Forests grow in the south and high north. The east and south contain rich farmland.

Rice terraces, such as these in Yunnan, can be found all over China.

4

Not only is China's land area large. With more than a billion people, it also has the largest population in the world. Most Chinese live in villages and work as farmers. But many people also live in cities, such as Shanghai, Beijing, and Hong Kong, and work in industry.

Farmers plowing fields with the help of oxen and workers weaving through busy city streets on bicycles are part of a culture that has existed for thousands of years. China has one of the world's oldest civilizations. Its history is divided into dynasties—periods of time ruled by emperors. This ancient country is known for its contributions to the world, such as paper, fireworks, compasses, and many other inventions. Its art and architecture, such as the written characters of calligraphy or traditional pagoda buildings, and even its food are reminders of a long past that is still an important part of China today.

Chinese city streets, such as these in Yibin, are often a hub of activity.

Nǐ chī fàn le méi? (Have You Eaten?)

You can visit many Chinese restaurants outside of China. As Chinese immigrants settled in Europe and the United States, they brought their traditional foods with them. In many cities around the world, there are large Chinese communities. In China itself, food has a long history tied to its traditions, land, and people.

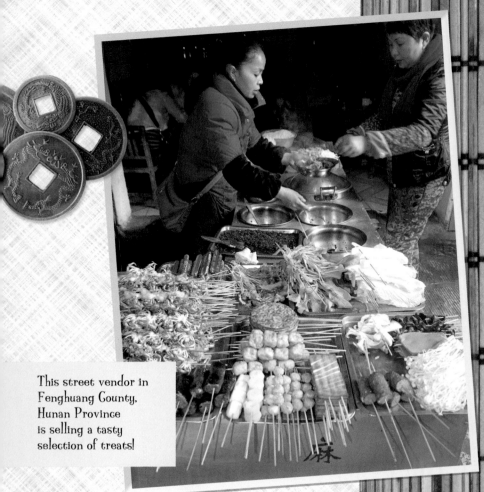

This street vendor in Fenghuang County, Hunan Province is selling a tasty selection of treats!

Different regions of China offer special foods. Cantonese cooking is probably the best known outside of the country. These stir-fried and steamed dishes offer lots of fresh flavors. Food from Sichuan and Hunan often contains bold spices from dried chili peppers and Sichuan peppercorns. In the east, coastal areas have access to lots of fresh fish. Rice is eaten all over the country. Wheat is also an important grain in the north, where it is used to make steamed breads, pancakes, and dumplings. The subtropical climate of the south provides lots of fruits and vegetables.

In China, people often share dishes at mealtimes. Platters in the center of the table hold a variety of meat and vegetable dishes. Guests serve themselves. The Chinese eat with chopsticks—two sticks that not only pick up bites of food, but can also be used to stir, mix, and serve food.

"Nǐ chī fàn le méi?" is a phrase the Chinese use to greet each other. It literally means "Have you eaten?"

Are you hungry for the fresh tastes of China?

Dumplings are a popular dish in China. Many people make them at home.

7

Chinese Ingredients

Here are some ingredients found in Chinese households and in the recipes in this book. If you can't find a certain ingredient, look for similar replacements.

Rice can be cooked in many different ways and is made into rice wine, rice vinegar, and rice flour. Chinese use long-grain rice as well as glutinous rice, also known as sticky rice, for sweet dishes and treats.

Soy is another basic Chinese ingredient. Soybeans are made into blocks of soft bean curd (tofu), bean pastes, soy milk, soy sauce, and many other products.

Noodles come in many varieties. Some are made with wheat flour and others with rice flour.

Vegetables include bok choy, watercress, baby corn, eggplant, broccoli, and winter melons. Some vegetables are picked young, such as bamboo shoots, bean sprouts, and pea pods. Root vegetables include ginger, water chestnuts, ginseng, lotus, taro, radish, and turnips. Garlic and scallions (also called spring onions or green onions) are both very common.

Chinese mushrooms include cloud ears, wood ears, black, straw, and shiitake.

Fruits include mandarin oranges, persimmons, pomelos, apples, pears, apricots, plums, dates, pineapples, lychees, and peaches.

Oils, such as peanut oil, are used to stir-fry meats and vegetables. Vegetable oil can also be used. Sesame oil adds a strong flavor. Chili oil, flavored with dried red chilies, adds a spicy bite.

Sauces are added to various dishes. Soy sauce comes in light and dark varieties. Plum sauce, oyster sauce, fish sauce, and hoisin sauce are also commonly used. Cornstarch, mixed with water, is used to thicken sauces.

Spices include dried red chili flakes, Sichuan peppercorns, cinnamon, and star anise. Chinese five-spice powder is a blend of cinnamon, cloves, Sichuan peppercorns, fennel, and star anise.

Fresh herbs include coriander leaves (also known as cilantro), lemongrass, and chives.

Nuts include peanuts, cashews, almonds, walnuts, chestnuts, and ginkgo nuts.

Meat in China often means pork. Beef is popular in the west, and lamb in the north. Chicken and duck are the common poultry.

Fish is caught fresh in both rivers and ocean. These include carp, eels, and shellfish such as crabs, shrimp, lobster, and scallops.

Wrappers, or thin sheets of dough, are sold to make wontons and other types of dumplings. Wontons and dumplings are pockets filled with meat or vegetables that can be steamed, fried, or boiled.

Drying and pickling are methods used to preserve some foods. These foods include dried red chilies, mushrooms, tangerine peel, seaweed, Sichuan pickles, and winter pickles.

Sweetness is added to dishes with white sugar, brown sugar, rock sugar (like rock candy), and honey. Sweetened red bean paste is used in buns and dumplings.

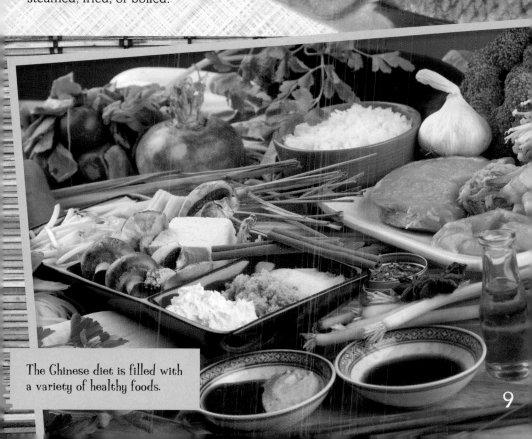

The Chinese diet is filled with a variety of healthy foods.

9

How to Use This Book

Each chapter of this book will introduce you to aspects of Chinese cooking. But you don't have to read the book from beginning to end. Flip through, find what interests you, and give it a try. You may discover a recipe that becomes your new favorite meal!

If you already do a lot of cooking, you may know your way around the kitchen. But if you've never stir-fried ginger, folded a wonton, or flipped a pancake, don't worry. Check out the glossary on page 44.

Zǎoshàng hǎo (Good Morning)

Before heading out to school or work for the day, Chinese families might eat rice porridge, one of the most popular morning meals. Others might eat an egg or a pancake with a glass of soy milk. These morning treats are also enjoyed as side dishes or snacks at other times of the day.

Congee Congee is a porridge made of rice. The rice cooks for a long time so the grains break up into a soft, thick soup. Congee is a comfort food in China. People may eat it to help them feel better when they are sick.

Ingredients	Tools
½ cup jasmine rice	Stockpot
4 cups water	Mixing spoon

16

Each recipe is set up the same way: Ingredients lists all the ingredients you'll need for the recipe. Tools tells you the various kitchen utensils you will need. Collect the ingredients and tools before you start working so that you have everything nearby when you need it.

Then just follow the Steps. Be sure to read them carefully. Numbers on the photos indicate which step they refer to. Don't worry if your creation isn't perfect when you reach the end. Cooking takes practice and experimentation. Be patient and enjoy the process.

Steps

1. Combine the rice and water in a stockpot. Bring to a boil. Then reduce the heat to low.

2. Cook covered for about 60 to 90 minutes, until the rice breaks down and softens. Stir frequently to prevent the rice from sticking to the bottom of the pot. Serve warm.

Quick Tip

Eating with chopsticks can be tricky. But the more you practice, the easier it will get.

- Hold the top chopstick with the tips of your thumb and index finger
- Hold the bottom stick between the tips of your middle and ring finger.
- Open and close the chopsticks with your index finger.

VARIATION

Congee can be eaten plain, but usually condiments are added. You can cook the rice in vegetable or chicken broth instead of water. Top it with pieces of cooked chicken or fish, or bite-size vegetables. Sichuan pickled vegetables are one of the most popular toppings (see recipe on page 26).

Dairy free **V**egetarian **V**egan **G**luten free

Makes 2 servings
Time: 60 to 90 minutes

If you have to follow a specific diet, or have food allergies, look for the labels on each recipe. These will tell you if a dish is vegan, vegetarian, dairy-free, gluten-free, or if it contains nuts. However, you should always check food packaging before use to be sure.

Nuts contains

Dairy free

Gluten free

Vegetarian

Vegan

Look at Quick Tips for cooking and kitchen advice, and Variations for swapping out ingredients for others if you would like.

Anytime you are in the kitchen, ask an adult to help or be nearby. You shouldn't use any knife or appliance without an adult's permission and assistance. Check out page 14 for more ways to be safe while you cook.

A Healthy Kitchen

It's fun to head out on a food adventure by trying new tastes from countries beyond your own. But you should also keep your health in mind. According to ChooseMyPlate.gov, the following are the basic food groups. The Chinese include these groups in a meal, or over the course of a day, to get the proper balance of nutrients to grow and be healthy.

Fruits and Vegetables

Fruit in China, from mandarin oranges to Asian pears, are enjoyed as a sweet flavor in a balanced meal. Vegetables are also a very important part of the Chinese diet. They are cooked in stir-fries and used as dumpling fillings. Both fruits and vegetables can help reduce your risk for certain diseases. They contain nutrients your body needs and fiber to keep your digestive system running smoothly.

MyPlate shows us the importance of eating a combination of all the food groups in our diets.

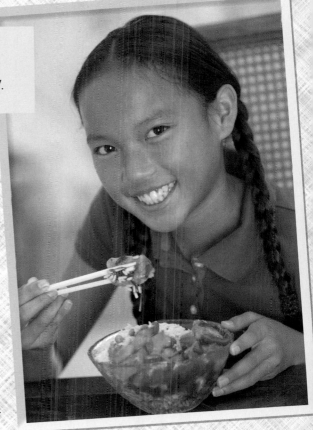

Try eating your Chinese meals with chopsticks! See how to use them on page 17.

Grains

These are foods made from wheat, rice, corn, or other grains. Whole grains that use the entire grain kernel are the healthiest. Refined grains, such as white flour and white rice, do not have as many vitamins and minerals. Rice is the main grain of China. Wheat is also a part of Chinese cuisine.

Protein

Protein foods include meat, poultry, seafood, and eggs. The Chinese also get protein from soy and nuts.

Dairy

Milk and any products made of milk fall into this category. Dairy foods contain a lot of bone-building calcium. The Chinese, however, do not normally eat dairy products. But they do get calcium from many sources, such as leafy green vegetables, oranges, almonds, sesame seeds, and soybeans.

Fats and Sugar

Some oils, especially the ones from plants like peanut, vegetable, and sesame oil, do provide some important nutrients. Nuts are high in oils, too. But solid fats, such as meat fat, are not as good for you. So use them sparingly. Your body needs sugar, but not too much. Try not to fill up on too many Chinese treats with added sugar.

A Safe Kitchen

It's fun to whip up a tasty new creation in the kitchen, but safety should be your number one concern. Here are some tips to keep in mind:

- Make sure an adult is nearby for permission, help, advice, and assistance.

- Wash your hands before you work.

- Wear the right clothing, including sturdy shoes and an apron.

- Foods can grow harmful bacteria. Be sure to keep foods in the refrigerator or freezer until they are ready to use. Check expiration dates. If something smells or looks funny, it may be spoiled.

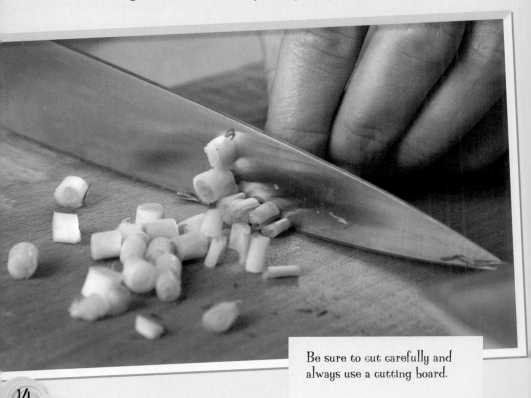

Be sure to cut carefully and always use a cutting board.

- Raw meat, poultry, seafood, and eggs can carry germs. Always wash your hands immediately after touching them. Wash any knife or cutting board after you use them and before you use them again. Make sure these foods are cooked all the way through before you eat them. Clean countertops and kitchen tools with warm, soapy water when you are done working.

- On the stovetop, be sure pot handles don't stick out, so the pots don't get knocked over. Never leave pots unattended. Do not let anything flammable, such as loose sleeves or kitchen towels, near burners on the stove.

Remember to rinse fruits and vegetables before you use them.

- Always use oven mitts when removing a pan from the oven or microwave. Avoid steam when you lift a top off a pot on the stove or in the oven.

- Knives are sharp. Always point the blade away from you. Take your time and pay attention to what you are cutting. Don't use a knife without the help of an adult.

Zǎoshàng hǎo (Good Morning)

Before heading out to school or work for the day, Chinese families might eat rice porridge, one of the most popular morning meals. Others might eat an egg or a pancake with a glass of soy milk. These morning treats are also enjoyed as side dishes or snacks at other times of the day.

Congee

Congee is a porridge made of rice. The rice cooks for a long time so the grains break up into a soft, thick soup. Congee is a comfort food in China. People may eat it to help them feel better when they are sick.

Ingredients

½ cup jasmine rice
4 cups water

Tools

Stockpot
Mixing spoon

Steps

1. Combine the rice and water in a stockpot. Bring to a boil. Then reduce the heat to low.

2. Cook covered for about 60 to 90 minutes, until the rice breaks down and softens. Stir frequently to prevent the rice from sticking to the bottom of the pot. Serve warm.

Quick Tip

Eating with chopsticks can be tricky. But the more you practice, the easier it will get.

- Hold the top chopstick with the tips of your thumb and index finger.

- Hold the bottom stick between the tips of your middle and ring finger.

- Open and close the chopsticks with your index finger.

Variation

Congee can be eaten plain, but usually condiments are added. You can cook the rice in vegetable or chicken broth instead of water. Top it with pieces of cooked chicken or fish, or bite-size vegetables. Sichuan pickled vegetables are one of the most popular toppings (see recipe on page 26).

Dairy free   **V**egetarian   **V**egan   **G**luten free

Makes 2 servings
Time: 60 to 90 minutes

Scallion Pancakes

Each bite of these round, savory treats is packed with scallions. Scallions (also called spring onions or green onions) are often used in Chinese cooking. The green ends used in this dish should be sliced thin to create little rings. You can serve these pancakes with soy sauce for dipping.

Ingredients

2 cups flour

1 teaspoon salt

1 cup boiling water

4 to 5 scallions, thinly sliced, green parts only

1 tablespoon sesame oil (for brushing)

1 tablespoon peanut oil (for frying)

Tools

Bowl

Mixing spoon

Measuring cups and spoons

Damp towel

Rolling pin

Pastry brush

Skillet

Turner

Knife

Cutting board

Baking sheet

Steps

1. Mix the flour and salt in a large bowl. Add ½ cup of the boiling water, stirring well. Add the rest of the water a little at a time. Let it cool slightly, and then use your hands to shape the dough into a ball.

2. Turn the dough out onto a floured surface and knead it for about a minute until smooth. Cover it with a damp towel and let it rest for about 30 minutes.

3. Sprinkle flour on your work surface and knead the dough about 10 times. Then cut it into 4 equal pieces.

4. With the rolling pin, roll one piece of the dough out into a thin disk. Brush it with sesame oil. Sprinkle with chopped scallions.

5. Starting at one end of the disk, roll the dough up into a tube shape. Then coil the tube into a circle.

6. Flatten the coil with your hand and roll it out with the rolling pin again into a thin, flat disc, about 6 to 7 inches across.

7. Heat the peanut oil in a skillet on medium high. Fry the pancake on one side for 1 to 2 minutes. Flip over with a turner, and cook on the other side for 1 or 2 minutes. Set on a baking sheet in an oven set at 200°F to keep warm while you cook the rest of the pancakes.

8. Cut into wedges to serve.

Makes 4 servings
Time: About 1 hour

Quick Tip

To measure the right amount of flour, spoon the flour into the measuring cup so that it mounds above the rim. With the flat edge of a butter knife, swipe across the top of the cup so the flour is level with the rim. This keeps the flour from being too packed into the cup.

N contains Nuts   **V**egan

Dairy free   **V**egetarian

Tea Eggs

The Chinese have been drinking tea for thousands of years. The flavor of tea is also a nice addition to eggs. Your kitchen will fill with the aromas of China while the eggs steep in a fragrant mixture. Tea eggs are sold at convenience stores throughout the country.

Ingredients

6 large eggs
Water for boiling
1 quart water for steeping
Leaves from 2 black tea bags
1/3 cup soy sauce
1 tablespoon white sugar
1 cinnamon stick
2 star anise

Tools

Stockpot
Spoon or fork
Measuring cups and spoons

Steps

1. Place the eggs in a stockpot and fill with water so all the eggs are covered. Bring to a boil. Reduce the heat, cover, and let simmer about 12 minutes.

2. Pour the hot water out of the pot, and fill again with cold water. Repeat until the eggs are cool enough to handle.

3. Lightly tap the eggs all over with the back of a spoon or fork. This will make small cracks all around the eggs, but the shells will still be attached to the eggs.

4. Refill the stockpot with 1 quart of fresh water. Add the soy sauce, tea, sugar, cinnamon, and star anise. Place the eggs into this mixture.

5. Heat to boiling over high heat, then reduce the heat and simmer uncovered for about 2 hours.

6. Drain the eggs, rinse to cool, and unpeel the shells to reveal the cracked patterns beneath.

 Gluten free **V**egetarian **D**airy free

Makes 3 servings (2 eggs each)
Time: About 2½ hours

Small Bites

The Chinese often sit down to three meals a day. But they also enjoy small bites in between. Street vendors sell snacks of meat, bowls of soup, or a plate of dumplings. Before a meal, a host might place some small snacks on the table, such as peanuts. During a meal, condiments, such as pickled vegetables, can be added to a dish.

Five-Spice Peanuts

There are five basic tastes in Chinese food: salty, sweet, sour, spicy, and bitter. This recipe combines this variety of flavors into one snack by using Chinese five-spice powder. A popular snack in China, peanuts are often boiled or fried. Here, they are baked.

Ingredients	Tools
2 tablespoons five-spice powder	Resealable plastic bag
½ teaspoon salt	Measuring cups and spoons
1 egg white, beaten	Bowl
1 teaspoon orange zest	Mixing spoon
2 cups unsalted roasted peanuts	Whisk
Nonstick cooking spray	Baking sheet
	Spatula

Steps

1. Preheat oven to 325°F.

2. In a resealable plastic bag, combine the five-spice powder, salt, and orange zest.

3. In a bowl, beat the egg white with a whisk. Add the nuts and stir well until the nuts are moist.

4. Pour the nuts into the bag of spices. Seal the bag, and shake it to evenly coat the nuts with spices.

5. Spray a baking sheet with nonstick cooking spray. Pour the nuts onto the baking sheet so they form a single layer.

6. Bake for about 20 to 25 minutes. Halfway through baking, swish the nuts around with a spatula to be sure they aren't sticking.

7. Allow to cool before serving.

Makes 2 cups
Time: About 30 minutes

Quick Tip

Orange zest is the skin of an orange. To zest an orange for this recipe, rub a grater with small holes across the skin to grate it into tiny strips.

Nuts contains

Gluten free

Dairy free

Vegetarian

Variations

You can make this snack with other popular Chinese nuts, such as cashews or walnuts.

Barbeque Spareribs

This Cantonese dish is prepared by roasting pork ribs that are slathered in a sweet, smoky sauce. Here, we use a slow cooker to help the ribs absorb the flavors and make the meat tender. Broiling them briefly before and after helps add a crisp layer.

Ingredients	Sauce	Tools
3 pounds country style ribs	½ cup hoisin sauce	Knife
	3 tablespoons soy sauce	Cutting board
Nonstick cooking spray	3 tablespoons honey	Broiling pan
	3 tablespoons rice vinegar	Bowl
	2 teaspoons sesame oil	Whisk
	3 garlic cloves, chopped	Baking dish
	½ teaspoon salt	Tongs
	½ teaspoon pepper	Baster
	1 cup chicken broth	Aluminum foil

Steps

1. If not already divided, cut the meat into individual ribs.

2. Spray the broiling pan with nonstick spray. Place the ribs on the pan, and broil on the top rack of the oven for about 15 minutes, flipping once during cooking, to brown the outside.

3. Meanwhile, in a bowl, whisk together the sauce ingredients.

4. Place the ribs in a baking pan. Pour about half of the sauce over the ribs. Set the oven to 350°F. Place the ribs on the center rack of the oven.

5. Cook the ribs for 3 hours, uncovered for the first 1½ hours and covered with foil the second 1½ hours. Every 30 minutes during cooking, flip the ribs over with tongs, and baste them with sauce. Add a little more sauce each time to keep the ribs from drying out.

Makes 6 to 8 servings as an appetizer
Time: 15 minutes prep, 3 hours cooking

luten
free

airy
free

6. If you want to make these ribs into a meal, serve with rice (see Quick Tip on page 33) and cucumber sticks.

25

Sichuan Pickled Vegetables

The people of Sichuan pickle vegetables by preserving them in vinegar and spices. Pickled vegetables add a spicy kick to mild dishes, such as congee, or a burst of flavor to other meals. If you can't find Sichuan peppercorns, you can use black peppercorns. The flavor is different, but they will still add heat to your pickles!

Ingredients

1 cucumber	2 slices fresh ginger root
5 radishes	2 teaspoons salt
1 cup shredded cabbage	1 teaspoon sugar
½ cup rice vinegar	½ teaspoon red chili flakes
½ cup water, plus more for filling	1 teaspoon Sichuan peppercorns

Tools

Knife
Cutting board
Measuring cups and spoons
Bowl
Mixing spoon
1 (32-ounce) empty pickle jar with lid (or a few smaller sized jars)
Saucepan
Vegetable peeler

Steps

1. Peel and seed the cucumber. Cut into 1-inch strips. Slice the radishes into small pieces. Combine in a bowl. Add the shredded cabbage. Stir to combine.

2. Fill the jar (or jars) to the top with the vegetable mixture.

3. In a small saucepan, heat the water, vinegar, ginger slices, salt, sugar, red chili flakes, and peppercorns. Bring to a boil. Stir until the sugar and salt are dissolved, a few minutes.

4. Pour the heated mixture into the jar (or divide the mixture among the jars) over the vegetables. Keep the ginger slices in the jar, too, to add flavor.

5. Add cold water until all of the vegetables are covered with liquid. Stir it with a spoon.

6. Let the jar cool, uncovered, to room temperature. Then twist on the lid and refrigerate the pickles for at least 24 hours before eating. They will get spicier the longer they sit. Serve with congee (see recipe on page 15), or alongside any Chinese dish as a condiment.

 Gluten free **D**airy free **V**egetarian **V**egan

Makes 1 (32-ounce) jar of vegetables

Time: About 20 minutes, at least 24 hours in the refrigerator. Eat within a week.

27

Vegetable Wonton Soup

Wontons are dumplings filled with pork, shrimp, or vegetables. Wontons can be boiled, steamed, or deep-fried. To eat them in a soup, bring the bowl close to your mouth, and use your chopsticks to hold the wonton to take a bite. You can sip the soup right from the bowl.

Ingredients

Wontons

1 package wonton wrappers
2 cups shredded cabbage
1 cup shredded carrots
1 cup sliced mushrooms
4 to 5 scallions, thinly sliced, white parts
¼ cup minced water chestnuts

2 teaspoons minced ginger root
½ teaspoon rice wine vinegar
½ teaspoon sesame oil
¼ teaspoon sugar
¼ teaspoon salt

Soup

4 cups chicken broth
2 slices fresh ginger root
4 to 5 scallions, thinly sliced, green parts
½ teaspoon sesame oil

Tools

Measuring cups and spoons
Stockpot
Slotted spoon
Colander
Paper towels
Knife
Cutting board
Bowl
Plastic wrap
Spoon
Baking sheet
Ladle
Four serving bowls
Greaseproof paper

Steps

1. In a stockpot, bring about 2 quarts of water to a boil. Add the cabbage, carrots, and sliced mushrooms. Return to a boil, then remove the vegetables with a slotted spoon into a bowl. Immediately rinse with cold water.

2. Wrap the drained vegetables in paper towels and squeeze to remove all the liquid. Place the vegetables on a cutting board and chop very finely.

3. Combine the chopped vegetables, white scallions, water chestnuts, and ginger in a bowl. Add the vinegar, sesame oil, sugar, and salt, and mix well. Cover with plastic wrap and refrigerate for about 30 minutes.

4. To fill the wontons, spoon a little of the filling into the center of a wonton wrapper. Dip your finger in water and run along the edges to wet the wrapper. Fold the wrapper in half and squeeze all around the edges to seal.

5. Wet one of the corners and tuck it under the opposite one. Squeeze to seal. Place the wontons on a parchment-lined baking sheet and cover with a damp paper towel to stop them from drying out.

6. Fill a stockpot halfway with water and bring to a boil. Add the wontons. When they float to the top, they are cooked. It will take about 3 minutes. Place a few in each serving bowl.

7. For the soup, bring the chicken broth and the sliced ginger to a boil in the stockpot. Lower heat and simmer for about 5 minutes.

8. Add the sesame oil. Ladle the broth over the wontons. Sprinkle with scallion greens to finish.

**Makes about 30 wontons
(4 to 6 servings)
Time: About 2 hours total**

Dairy free

The Ancient Wok

The wok is the basic piece of cooking equipment that has been used in China for thousands of years. Chinese people use the wok for one of the most popular and quickest methods of cooking—stir-frying. To stir-fry, you cook ginger, garlic, vegetables, and meat in a little oil, constantly stirring and tossing them while they cook. You can add sauces and spices as you go. Stir-frying helps keep the vegetables colorful, crispy, fresh, and nutritious.

If you don't have a wok, you can use a skillet instead. Be careful, though. Oil can splatter and burn if you don't pay close attention while you are cooking.

Kung Pao Chicken

The origin of Kung Pao chicken is uncertain. One legend says that it was the favorite dish of a Sichuan governor in the late 1800s. It is said that after trying the dish, he liked it so much that he had it named after him! Whatever the case, this is a delicious dish, and remains one of the most popular Chinese dishes outside of China.

Ingredients

1 pound boneless chicken breasts, cut into ½-inch cubes

2 teaspoons cornstarch mixed with 1 tablespoon water

1 teaspoon rice wine vinegar

1 tablespoon peanut oil

5 to 6 scallions, thinly sliced, white parts only

4 garlic cloves, minced

2 teaspoons minced ginger root

About 8 to 10 dried red chilies, seeded (or ½ teaspoon red chili flakes)

1/3 cup unsalted dry roasted peanuts

Sauce

2 teaspoons soy sauce

2 teaspoons Chinese black vinegar (or balsamic vinegar)

1 teaspoon sesame oil

2 teaspoons sugar

1 teaspoon ground Sichuan pepper

Tools

Measuring cups and spoons
Bowl
Whisk
Skillet
Mixing spoon

Steps

1. In a bowl, whisk together the cornstarch, water, and rice vinegar. Add the chicken pieces and mix until well coated. Set aside to marinate for about 15 minutes.

2. In another bowl, whisk together the sauce ingredients.

3. Heat the peanut oil in the skillet. Add the marinated chicken and stir-fry for about 3 to 4 minutes until it cooks through.

4. Add the scallions, garlic, ginger, and red chilies. Stir-fry for 45 seconds.

5. Add the sauce and stir well so the chicken is coated. Sprinkle in the peanuts and stir to combine. Serve with rice (see Quick Tip on page 33).

Quick Tip

Cutting meat into small, bite-size pieces makes it cook quickly, and also makes it easier to pick up with chopsticks. Kitchen scissors can be used to cut the meat.

Ncontains uts   **D**airy free   **G**luten free

Makes 4 servings
Time: About 30 minutes

Sweet and Sour Pork

The Chinese have an ancient belief that yin and yang (forces in the universe) must be in balance. Mixing various flavors and textures in a dish or a meal makes it a balanced meal. This could be a mix of cool and warm flavors, or soft and crunchy textures. The opposite tastes of sweet and sour are in balance in this classic dish.

Ingredients

¾ pound pork tenderloin, cut into ½-inch strips

½ cup flour

Salt and pepper, to taste

2 tablespoons peanut oil, divided

6 to 7 scallions, thinly sliced, white parts only

1 red pepper, seeded and cut into squares

2 garlic cloves, minced

1 teaspoon minced ginger root

1 teaspoon cornstarch mixed with ½ tablespoon water

1 (20-ounce) can pineapple chunks in juice

Sauce

2 tablespoons soy sauce

3 tablespoons white distilled vinegar

3 tablespoons brown sugar

1 teaspoon sesame oil

2 tablespoons tomato paste

½ cup pineapple juice (from the canned pineapple chunks)

Tools

Measuring cups and spoons

Bowls

Whisk

Skillet

Mixing spoon

Steps

1. In a bowl, toss together the flour and salt and pepper. Add the pork pieces and toss with the flour until well coated. Set aside.

2. Whisk together the sauce ingredients. Set aside.

3. In the skillet, heat 1 tablespoon peanut oil. Add the pork and stir-fry until mostly cooked through, about 3 to 4 minutes. Remove the pork from the skillet and set aside.

4. Heat another tablespoon of peanut oil in the skillet. Add the scallions and red pepper. Stir-fry for 2 minutes. Add the ginger and garlic and stir-fry for about 1 more minute.

5. Add the pineapple chunks and the sauce. Bring to a boil. Add the pork back in, and let it all cook together for another 2 minutes.

6. Stir in the cornstarch and water mixture. Cook for another minute or until the pork is cooked through and the sauce has thickened. Serve with rice (see Quick Tip, right).

Quick Tip

Rice is the perfect addition to a stir-fry dish. Rice helps balance an especially spicy dish. It also absorbs the sauce.

To make rice, follow the directions on the package. You may need to rinse the rice first, to wash off the extra starch. Keep the lid on the saucepan while the rice absorbs the water. Before serving, fluff it with chopsticks to separate the grains.

Makes 4 servings
Time: About 20 minutes

Tofu with Pea Pods and Bamboo Shoots

Some Chinese dishes use bean curd (tofu) as the main protein instead of meat. Tofu does not have a lot of flavor on its own. It absorbs the flavors it is cooked with. This stir-fry dish also uses tasty vegetables—the young, tender shoots of bamboo and crispy, green pea pods.

Ingredients

1 (14-ounce) package medium-firm tofu, drained

5 to 6 scallions, thinly sliced, white and green parts separated

2 teaspoons minced ginger root

1 (8-ounce) can bamboo shoots, rinsed and drained

1 cup pea pods

1 tablespoon peanut oil

2 teaspoons cornstarch mixed with 1 tablespoon water

Sauce

1 tablespoon soy sauce

½ cup vegetable stock

1 teaspoon brown sugar

Tools

Knife

Cutting board

Measuring cups and spoons

Whisk

Skillet

Mixing spoon or turner

Steps

1. Cut the tofu into ½-inch cubes. Prepare the scallions, ginger, bamboo shoots, and pea pods. Whisk together the sauce ingredients. Set aside.

2. Heat the peanut oil in the skillet. Add the ginger and white parts of the scallions. Stir-fry for about 1 minute.

3. Add the cubes of tofu. Stir-fry them for another 2 minutes, stirring gently.

4. Add the bamboo shoots and pea pods. Stir-fry for another minute.

5. Add the sauce and stir to coat. Pour in the cornstarch and water mixture. Cook for another minute, gently stirring until the sauce thickens slightly.

6. Sprinkle with the green parts of the scallions. Serve with rice (see Quick Tip on page 33).

Quick Tip

Stir-frying is a quick process. That's why it's important to prepare all of your ingredients ahead of time. Before you heat the oil, cut your vegetables and meat or tofu, and mix your sauces. Then they are ready to add when you need them.

VARIATION

If you are not a fan of bamboo shoots or pea pods, you can add any vegetable you want to this dish. Try broccoli, baby corn, or bok choy. Toss in water chestnuts to add a fresh crunch.

Vegetarian **N**contains uts

Vegan **D**airy free **G**luten free

Makes 4 to 6 servings with rice
Time: About 15 minutes

Fàn and Miàn (Rice and Noodles)

Rice (called *fàn*) is a handy ingredient in Chinese cuisine. It can be served for breakfast, lunch, dinner, and snacks. It can be steamed, boiled, and fried. Noodles (*miàn*) are also an easy base for vegetables, meat, and flavorings.

Fried Rice

Fried rice is a Cantonese dish. It's a quick and easy way to make a meal using leftovers. Peas are used here, but you can add any type of small, diced vegetable.

Ingredients

- 1 teaspoon & 1 tablespoon vegetable oil, divided
- 2 eggs, beaten
- 3 thin slices fresh ginger root
- ½ cup frozen green peas, thawed
- ½ cup finely diced cooked ham
- ½ teaspoon sugar
- 2 tablespoons soy sauce
- 3 cups cooked rice
- 2 scallions, thinly sliced
- Black pepper, to taste

Tools

- Skillet
- Mixing spoon
- Whisk

Steps

1. Heat 1 teaspoon of oil in the skillet. Add the beaten eggs. Scramble them for about 1 minute, breaking them into small bits as you cook. Remove from the skillet and set aside.

2. Heat 1 tablespoon of oil in the skillet. Add the ginger and peas. Stir-fry for about 1 minute.

3. Add the ham, sugar, and soy sauce. Stir-fry for about 2 minutes.

4. Stir in the rice and fry for about 2 more minutes.

5. Take the skillet off the heat. Add the cooked eggs and scallions. Add pepper to taste.

Quick Tip

To beat an egg, break the egg into a bowl. With a fork or a whisk, stir quickly in a circular motion until the yolk and white are fully blended together.

Dairy free

Gluten free

Makes 4 servings
Time: About 30 minutes

Dan Dan Noodles

Dan dan noodles are a traditional street food in Sichuan. They get their name from the bamboo poles, called *dan*, that vendors wear over their shoulders. Hanging from these poles are baskets holding the pots, stoves, and sauces used to make the noodles.

Ingredients

1 (10-ounce) package Chinese noodles
1 tablespoon peanut oil
1 teaspoon minced ginger root
2 garlic cloves, minced
8 ounces ground pork
Salt

Sauce

2 tablespoons soy sauce
1 teaspoon sesame oil
2 teaspoons rice vinegar
¼ teaspoon red chili flakes (or more if you like it spicy!)
½ teaspoon Sichuan pepper
½ teaspoon sugar
3 to 4 scallions, thinly sliced, green parts only

Tools

Measuring spoons
Knife
Cutting board
Stockpot
Mixing spoon
Colander
Large bowl
Small bowl
Whisk
4 serving bowls
Skillet

Steps

1. In a stockpot, cook the noodles according to the package directions. Drain and rinse with cold water. Set aside.

2. In a large bowl, whisk together the sauce ingredients. Add the cooled noodles to the sauce and toss to coat. Set aside.

3. In a skillet, heat the peanut oil on a high heat. Add the ginger and garlic and cook for about 1 minute. Add the pork and cook for about 10 minutes until brown and crispy. Add salt to taste.

4. Place a serving of noodles in each bowl. Top the noodles with the pork.

Quick Tip

Mincing means to cut an ingredient into tiny pieces. To make mincing ginger and garlic easier, you can use a grater with small holes instead of a knife. The grater will mince the ginger and garlic for you. But be careful of your fingers when you get near the end.

Dairy free

N contains uts

VARIATION

Dan dan noodles are known for their spiciness. You can control the heat with the amount of red chili flakes. You can also serve something cooling alongside, such as cucumbers, in case your mouth gets too hot!

Makes 4 servings
Time: About 30 minutes

Chinese Sweets

At Chinese restaurants outside of China, you might crack open a fortune cookie at the end of a meal. But fortune cookies are not actually eaten in China. In fact, most meals don't end in dessert as we think of it. Sweet soups and other dishes may be part of the actual meal. Or they may be reserved for special occasions and holidays. Fruit is the "sweet" most often eaten at the end of a meal.

Steamed Pears

Steaming is a traditional Chinese method of cooking. Food becomes soft and soothing as it cooks in the steam of boiling water. In a traditional Chinese kitchen, cooks use steamers made of bamboo that can be stacked on top of a wok filled with boiling water. You can make a steamer with various bits of equipment you may already have around the kitchen.

Ingredients	Tools	
2 Asian pears	Steamer (see Quick Tip)	Cutting board
2 tablespoons honey	Measuring spoons	Melon baller
2 tablespoons chopped dates	Bowl	
	Knife	

Steps

1. Add water to your steamer and bring to a boil.

2. Wash the pears gently under cold water. If they can't stand upright on their own, cut a small piece off the bottom to make them flat. Then cut about ⅓ off the top of each pear. Set the tops aside.

3. With a melon baller, scoop out the seeds and cores to make small "wells" in the middle of each pear. Be careful not to break through the bottoms.

4. Mix the honey and dates together in a bowl. Spoon into the wells in the pears. Cover with the tops of the pears.

5. Place your pears in the steamer. Cover and turn the heat down to medium-low. Steam for about 30 to 40 minutes, or until the pears are soft when poked with a fork.

Quick Tip

If you don't own a wok and bamboo steamer, you can use a large stockpot. Place a metal colander or steamer basket inside. Or make small holes in a disposable pie plate and place it on a cooling rack in the bottom of the pot.

Variation

Asian pears have a thick skin and are firm like apples. But if you can't find them in your grocery store, try another pear variety, such as Bartlett, Anjou, or Bosc.

Gluten free

Dairy free

Vegetarian

Vegan

Makes 2 servings
Time: About 40 minutes

Almond Cookies

These crunchy cookies, called *hang jan beng* in Cantonese, are sold in bakeries in China and are a popular Chinese New Year treat.

Ingredients	Tools
2 cups flour	Measuring cups and spoons
¼ teaspoon salt	Large mixing bowl
½ teaspoon baking soda	Mixing spoon
1 cup sugar	Fork
1 cup vegetable shortening	Spoon
1 egg, lightly beaten	Baking sheet
2 teaspoons almond extract	Cooling rack
36 whole almonds	Turner

Steps

1. Preheat oven to 350°F.

2. In a large mixing bowl, combine the flour, salt, baking soda, and sugar.

3. Use a fork to combine the shortening with the dry ingredients. Use your hands to squeeze the mixture until it is crumbly.

4. Mix in the egg and almond extract. (Hands work best for this step, too.) Form the dough into a large ball.

5. Scoop out a tablespoon of dough. Roll it into a ball in your palms. Continue until you've used all the dough. Place the cookies about 2 inches apart on a baking sheet.

6. Gently flatten each cookie into a circle as you press an almond into the center.

7. Bake for 12 to 15 minutes until lightly browned on the edges. Remove from the oven and let cool slightly on the baking sheet for about 2 minutes. Then use a turner to move them to a cooling rack.

N^{contains}uts **D**airy free **V**egetarian

Makes 3 dozen cookies
Time: About 1 hour

Glossary

Tools

colander	round bowl-shaped tool with holes for draining foods
cutting board	flat work surface that protects counters from knife marks when cutting food
grater	flat metal tool with small blades used to cut foods into small strips
ladle	serving spoon with a bowl-shaped scoop
measuring cups and spoons	Dry measuring cups and spoons come in different sizes to help you measure accurate amounts. A liquid measuring cup is marked with lines along the side to measure liquids.
melon baller	tool used to scoop ball shapes out of fruit
saucepan	pan with a long handle, lid, and high sides for use on the stovetop
skillet	pan with a long handle and low sides for use on the stovetop; also called a frying pan
spatula	utensil used for mixing, spreading, or scraping the sides of pots and bowls
steamer	pan used to heat and cook foods with steam
stockpot	large, round metal pot for use on the stovetop with handles on each side and a lid
turner	utensil with a flat end used to flip food over or remove it from a pan
whisk	tool used to break down ingredients and bring air into a mixture

Terms

boil	heat a liquid until bubbles rise to the surface
condiment	food that adds additional flavor served alongside a dish
dice	cut into small pieces (smaller than chopping, but bigger than mincing)
knead	mix dough by folding it in half and flattening it with the heel of your hand
marinate	soak in a liquid and spices to add flavor
mince	cut into very fine pieces
savory	not sweet
shred	cut into strips
simmer	cook over low heat so that the liquid bubbles gently, but does not boil
steam	cook by heating with steam
steep	soak herbs or spices in a liquid to give the liquid flavor
stir fry	cook in oil on a very hot temperature
to taste	amount that tastes best to you
whisk	beat quickly with a whisk to break down ingredients and bring air into a mixture
zest	peel of an orange or other citrus fruit

Find Out More

Books

Catel, Patrick. *China*. Chicago: Heinemann, 2012.

Deady, Kathleen W. *Ancient China: Beyond the Great Wall*. Mankato, MN: Capstone, 2012.

Kuskowski, Alex. *Super Simple Chinese Art*. Minneapolis: ABDO, 2012.

Locricchio, Matthew. *The Cooking of China*. New York: Marshall Cavendish Benchmark, 2012.

Peppas, Lynn. *Cultural Traditions in China*. New York: Crabtree, 2012.

DVDs

Bompoint, Jean-Louis. *China*. Wynnewood, PA: Schlessinger Media, 2007.

Cooking with Kids: Celebrating Chinese New Year. San Francisco, CA: Ni Hao Productions, 2008.

Web Sites

KidsHealth: Being Safe in the Kitchen
http://kidshealth.org/kid/watch/house/safe_in_kitchen.html
Read tips to keep you safe as you cook.

MyPlate
www.choosemyplate.gov
This site describes a healthy, balanced way to get all the nutrients you need.

National Geographic Kids: China
http://kids.nationalgeographic.com/kids/places/find/china
View videos, look at maps, and read lots of information at this interactive site.

Time for Kids: China
www.timeforkids.com/destination/china
Visit this site to learn lots about one of the world's oldest and largest civilizations.

Further Research

If this book gave you a taste for Chinese food, there are many more Chinese cookbooks you could look at. You could also locate Chinese restaurants in your own town or city to try a bite of authentic Chinese dishes.

You may also be curious about China's history and culture. Stop into your local library and ask a librarian to help you learn more. Or ask a parent to help you look up Web sites for recipes, museums, or other information about China.

Index